W9-ACN-650

3 1242 00254 1515

J
636.7
CRI

Everything
DOG

What Kids Really Want to Know About Dogs

by
Marty Crisp

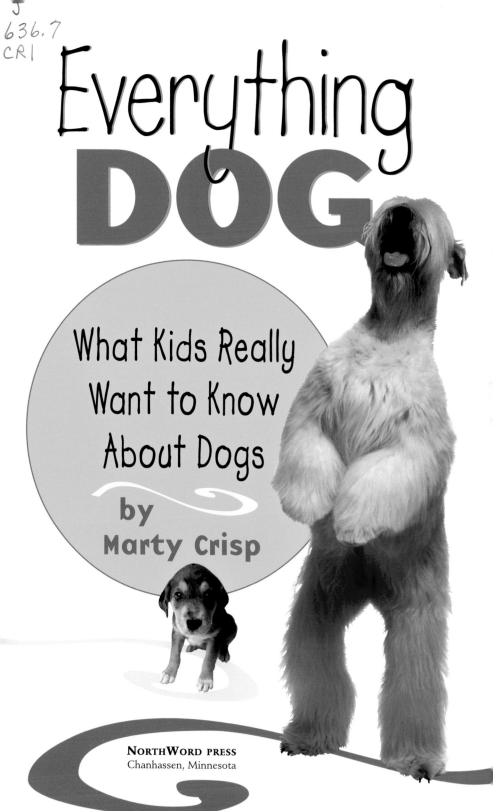

NorthWord press
Chanhassen, Minnesota

Edited by Ruth Strother
Cover and text design by Michele Lanci-Altomare

Text copyright © 2003 by Marty Crisp

Books for Young Readers
NorthWord Press
18705 Lake Drive East
Chanhassen, MN 55317
www.northwordpress.com

All rights reserved. No part of this work covered by the copyrights hereon
may be reproduced or used in any form or by any means—
graphic, electronic or mechanical, including photocopying, recording,
taping of information on storage and retrieval systems—
without the prior written permission of the publisher.

Photographs provided by Getty Images

Library of Congress Cataloging-in-Publication Data Pending

Crisp, Marty,
    Everything dog : what kids really want to know about dogs / by Marty
Crisp. P. cm. – (Kids' FAQs)
    Summary: Uses a question-and-answer format to present a variety of
Information about dogs.
    Includes bibliographical references and index.
    ISBN 13: 978 -1-55971-839-4 (hardcover) – ISBN 13: 978 -1-55971-854-7 (softcover)
1. Dogs—Miscellanea—Juvenile literature. [1. Dogs—Miscellanea. 2.
Questions and answers.] I. Title. II. Series

SF426.5C75 2002
636.7—dc21   2002032631

Printed in Huizhou, Guangdong,
PRC, China September 2014

Acknowledgments

THE AUTHOR WOULD LIKE TO ACKNOWLEDGE THE invaluable expertise of the vets and staff at Conestoga Animal Hospital, Hinkletown, PA; the vets and staff at Neffsville Veterinary Clinic, Neffsville, PA; and Paul J. Cappiello, DVM, Peaceable Kingdom Animal Hospital, 1735 W. Main St., Ephrata, PA.

Dedication

TO ALL THE KIDS EVERYWHERE WHO LOVE DOGS (and read dog books!). I feel the same way.

—*M. C.*

contents

From retriever to Dalmatian,
dogs and people form loving
relationships with each other.

introduction

THE RELATIONSHIP BETWEEN PEOPLE AND dogs is unique. We are two very different species, who have actually grown to love and trust each other. Despite this love, dogs are still a mystery to many people. I write fiction about dogs, so when I go on school visits, kids ask me questions about dogs. Over the years, I've collected these questions and researched their answers.

This book contains the answers to all the intriguing questions kids would like to ask their dogs but can't, because dogs don't talk. Not the way people do. Dogs talk using body language— the movement of ears and tails and snouts. They also use growls, whimpers, barks, howls, and, in some cases, yodels. Dogs can find out more about people with a few good sniffs than people can find out about dogs after hours of observation. Here's your chance to take a good sniff of everything dog. Let's start at the beginning and find out where this remarkable creature called dog came from.

Do dogs come from dinosaurs?

Not from the reptiles you see on the movie screen in *Jurassic Park*. There are no *T. Rexes* or *Velociraptors* in the dog's background. Dinosaurs disappeared 65 million years ago. Dogs date back only 30 million years to the Oligocene period, when a long, low, mongooselike creature appeared. Scientists today call him *Cynodictis*. He had teeth that could be used for both crushing and chewing. These special teeth are now called canines, meaning of or relating to dogs. Even people have canines, also known as eyeteeth. These are our sharpest, most pointed teeth. In dogs (and in vampire movies), canines are also called fangs.

It took 6 million years more for *Cynodictis* to evolve, or change, into a creature called *Tomarctus*. This was a mammal who actually looked a bit like a dog. The word *"Tomarctus"* means "bear-dog" in Latin, and both dogs and bears can trace their origins to this early wolflike animal. It wasn't until about 300,000 years ago (which in geological time is just like yesterday, or, at least, last week), that one part of the *Tomarctus* line evolved into the group *Canis*. This group includes *Canis lupus* (wolf) and *Canis familiaris* (dog). Like human beings, dogs and wolves live in family groups, called packs, helping and protecting each other.

The dog's ancestors first came on the scene about 12,000 to 10,000 years ago.

During the Ice Age, about 40,000 years ago, wild dogs first started hanging around human settlements, feasting on the hunters' leavings and sometimes getting warm by their fires. This may have been the only time in history that messy human garbage dumps resulted in something good. The dogs' keen noses brought them close to human camps, and dogs have been willing to help us clean up after ourselves ever since.

The first domestic dog appeared about 12,000 to 10,000 years ago. Through breeding and selection of special traits—such as speed and scenting ability—people have molded dogs into an amazing number of shapes and sizes, always trying to make our best friend even better.

Why do dogs like people?

Like wolves, dogs are pack animals. They like living in family groups, following a leader, and working together for the good of the whole pack. Prehistoric cave dwellers were the first people to notice that dogs are intelligent, with a superior sense of smell. They also noticed that dogs are excellent hunters and very fast on their four feet. Dogs apparently liked the cave dwellers' home cooking and the way people could scratch the unreachable parts of their backs. It was the beginning of a friendship that has endured for almost as long as people have existed on earth.

What can a dog tell by smelling a person, and what can a person tell by smelling a dog?

Dogs have amazing noses. While people have only 5 million scent receptors in their noses, dogs have over 200 million scent receptors in their noses and on the roofs of their mouths. Dogs also have a much larger olfactory, or smell, processing center in their brains than we do. That means dogs can figure out what they're smelling more easily than we can. Wolves and wild dogs needed good noses to track their prey and avoid danger. In the wild, dogs and wolves with the best noses survived and became more numerous.

Most domestic dogs still have keen noses. Flat-faced breeds such as bulldogs, however, have inferior smelling abilities, while long-faced hound dogs are the best smellers around. Some dogs are

even trained to sniff out cancer in humans, to predict epileptic seizures, and to find illegal substances humans are trying hard to hide. But it's almost impossible to hide anything that smells from a dog.

Whatever the breed, dogs can interpret what they're smelling with what seems like astounding accuracy to us weak-nosed humans. In fact, your dog can "read" you like a book. A dog can tell what you had for lunch, whom you hung out with, and which way you walked home from school. That's why a dog sniffs you all over when you come through the door. Mom might have to ask what you've been up to, but your dog already knows.

A human being's less-developed sense of smell provides only the big picture, not the details. We can tell when a dog has been in the rain (a wet smell), rolled in garbage (a yucky smell), or been to the doggy beauty parlor. (Dogs put up with the sweet spray-on canine cologne for the sake of their people. Dogs much prefer honest earthy smells—such as dried poop or dead mice.)

Can dogs recognize other people in your family by their smell?

Absolutely. Even when you're not actually dripping with sweat, you, and every human being, perspire all the time. And one gram of the butyric acid naturally found in human perspiration contains seven sextillion molecules of smell (that's an actual number, not a joke). That smell is genetically programmed in a person from birth. All your blood relatives carry a similar smell, even if they try to cover it up with bottles of perfume. That one gram of smell would be enough that even if it were in only one little spot on top of a ten-story building, your dog could find it. So it doesn't matter how much deodorant you or your relatives wear. Your dog's nose knows.

No matter how many baths you take, your dog can recognize you and your relatives by smell alone.

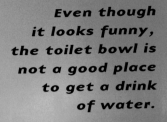

Even though it looks funny, the toilet bowl is not a good place to get a drink of water.

How do dogs drink
with their noses
in the water?

It only looks like they plunge their muzzles into their water bowls (or the toilet bowl) to drink. Dogs usually lap the water into their mouths with their noses hovering above the surface. A dog's tongue curls, acting like a spoon, and scoops up the water.

Why do some dogs' ears stick up while others flop down?

Nature designed the dog with triangular ears that stand up straight like a wolf's ears. Those stand-up ears form a cup that allows a dog to hear sounds four times farther away than a human can hear. Puppies, however, (including wolf puppies) are born with soft ears that flop over. People who develop dog breeds often select the floppy puppy-ear trait as a way to give a breed of dog an appealing babyish look. Drop-eared dogs such as the basset hound and the spaniel were developed to have this babyish look.

Dogs with erect ears can hear better than those with floppy ears. They can move their ears in the direction of sound to fine-tune their listening. Dogs with floppy ears, on the other hand, can usually smell better. The ears trail on the ground, sweeping smells into the nose.

Docked

Button

Dog ears come in all shapes and sizes: prick or erect ears (German shepherds); rose ears (bulldogs); button ears (fox terriers); pendant ears (Dalmatians); or bat ears (basenjis) are some of the official types. There was a time when slightly floppy-eared dogs such as boxers and Great Danes had their ears docked. Veterinarians would cut off the floppy part of these dogs' ears surgically. Some owners preferred their dogs with docked ears, mainly for reasons of appearance and to meet old breed standards. Docking has fallen into disfavor today. Most American vets have decided it's unnecessary and just don't do it anymore. In England, vets can't do it. It's against the law.

Prick

Dog ears come in many shapes from the spaniel's pendant ears (left) to the German shepherd's prick ears (right).

Pendant

Dog food looks and smells pretty gross, so why do dogs like it?

· · · · · · · · · ·

Can people eat dog food?

Dogs have far fewer taste buds than people: about one for every six we have. So dogs are not as picky about their food. What a dog wants is something strong-smelling since smell is the main way dogs enjoy their food. People can eat dog food, but we probably wouldn't like the ripe smell or the bland taste. Also, we don't have the right kind of teeth for smashing up hard chunks of dog kibble.

This Labrador retriever's strong jaws and pointy cusps make eating hard kibble easy.

Dogs have a sturdier hinge on their jaw than we have, and that gives their bite more power. Like wolves, dogs have the ability to bite down hard and hang onto prey that is still moving. A dog's teeth also have better cusps, or sharp points, on their otherwise flat molars. A human's molars are rounded. A dog's cusps act as chisels to crack kibble easily.

Are there any diseases people can get from dogs or dogs can get from people?

People cannot get most viruses or bacterial infections from dogs and vice versa. Most viruses and bacterial infections are what doctors call species specific, and dogs are a completely different species from people. So we can't trade most diseases. We can, however, get parasites such as ringworms or mange mites from dogs. Also, rabies is a nasty virus that lives in a dog's saliva and can be passed to humans if the infected dog bites us.

How many hours a day is a dog supposed to sleep?

Sleep time varies greatly by age. Old dogs and young puppies sleep longer. But the average healthy adult pet dog probably sleeps about 16 hours a day. Your dog may sleep from 10 to 20 hours a day, depending on how busy he is. There are also differences among breeds when it comes to sleep. Working breeds such as Siberian huskies and corgis are more active and usually more high-strung. They sleep less. Lap dogs such as papillons and Pekingese sleep more.

When sleeping dogs twitch and make noises, are they dreaming?

No one knows for sure if dogs dream. But most experts believe dogs do dream about everything from chasing rabbits to greeting their people. Just like humans, dogs' eyelids sometimes tremble during REM sleep. REM stands for "rapid eye movement." For humans, REM sleep means dream time.

Sleeping dogs often twitch, jerk, and make noises that seem funny and make us wonder what they're dreaming about. Just like a person, a dog relaxes all his muscles during sleep. This is what leads both dogs and people to snort, grunt, and make other silly noises in their sleep.

Some dogs, such as the boxer on the opposite page, may even sleep with their eyes open.

Do dogs ever
fall in love?

A dog does not mate for life with just one other dog. But dogs are faithful to their fellow pack members. Many dogs seem to choose one person to whom they give all their love and loyalty. Some dogs, such as chow chows and Scottish terriers, are strictly one-person dogs and form particularly strong attachments to that person. Other dogs, especially floppy-eared dogs, keep the puppy trait of seeming to love everyone.

Dogs are faithful to their fellow pack members whether they are human or canine.

If things are going well in a human family, the dog will know that one of the people in the house is the alpha, or leader, of the pack. The dog will give that person a lot of respect and affection. A dog may decide all or some of his humans rank lower in the pack's pecking order than he does. That dog may elect himself the alpha, and growl and nip at his humans to try to get them to follow orders. It's exactly how the alpha male and female in a wolf pack treat their pack mates.

Being alpha is a bit like being president of the pack. If someone new seems stronger and smarter, a new alpha can be "elected." This behavior comes from the dog's wild ancestry and can be seen in wolves today. The male and female alpha wolves rule the pack. They mate year after year until new alphas win their way to the top.

Do dogs cry?

Dogs have lachrymal, or tear, glands, which constantly produce tears that wash the surface of their eyes. These glands sometimes get clogged up causing a discharge under a dog's eyes that makes him look like he's crying. But dogs don't express their sad emotions by shedding tears. They use body language (tail between legs, head down) or sounds (howls and whimpers). Dogs also express grief by lying around, moping, and not eating. They may grieve for anyone in their pack, human or dog, who dies or even just goes away. Dogs live completely in the present. They don't keep date books or look at calendars. When you're on vacation, they don't know you'll be back in a week. They only know you're gone.

A TV screen may
look about the
same to a dog
as a painting
looks to us.

How come my dog never seems to watch TV with me?

• • • • • • • • •

Can dogs see what people see?

Most dogs can see in an arc of 250 degrees. Humans (and flat-faced dogs such as the Pekingese) have only 180 degrees of vision. This means that dogs spend a lot of time seeing with either one eye or the other (this is called monocular vision while humans have binocular, or two-eyed, vision). That's why dogs are not as good as people are at picking out details or seeing colors. But they're much better at spotting movement, and their eyes work better than ours in dim light. Most dogs lack the detail vision needed to enjoy television. Many scientists believe that the flat screen looks about the same to a dog as a painting hanging on the wall looks to us.

Did anyone ever "invent" his or her own breed of dog?

Definitely. People have been creating their own breeds of dogs for years, trying to make "the perfect dog" who can do exactly what that person wants. For instance, a tax collector named Louis Doberman needed a dog to protect him as he made his rounds collecting taxes in nineteenth century Germany. So he selected the traits of the German shepherd, rottweiler, German pinscher, and Manchester terrier to get just the size, shape, and temperament he wanted in a dog. And he named the result (what else?) the Doberman!

Another "vanity" dog (think vanity license plates on cars) is the Jack Russell terrier, also called the Parson Jack Russell terrier. This dog was bred to be a hunting dog in England by (who else?) the Reverend John "Jack" Russell, who was nick-named The Hunting Parson by his congregation.

The Jack Russell is a small, agile, brave terrier developed to hunt foxes and raccoons. In 1870, Rev. Russell crossed wire-coated fox terriers with other terrier breeds, looking for intelligence, patience, and fearlessness. He came up with a winner because his breed remains popular today, sought after for its easy trainability and willingness to work.

Most breeds of dogs, such as the Jack Russell terrier at right, were developed for particular purposes.

The Molossus hound, one of the Great Dane's ancestors, is now extinct.

Have any dog breeds ever become extinct?

Yes, but only a few. It wasn't until the late 1800s that people started keeping a registry of breeds. Most modern breeds are descended from early breeds with general names such as water dog (used for dogs who like water, such as the Chesapeake

Bay retriever) or shock dog (used for dogs with a bushy shock of hair, such as the poodle).

A working terrier known as the turnspit disappeared in the early 1900s. It was an actual breed, recorded in dog reference books written in the sixteenth to nineteenth centuries. Turnspits were described as ugly little dogs with bowed legs, long bodies, and large heads. They were run in large wooden wheels (think hamsters) to turn a crank that turned a spit where meat was roasted over a fire. Before these dogs became extinct, people in rural areas without electricity used turnspits to run on treadmills that powered devices such as washing machines and butter churns. But nobody was interested in keeping this breed going once electricity became available to everyone.

Another extinct breed is the legendary Molossian from the heyday of the Roman Empire. Used to hunt wild boar, bait bulls, and fight alongside Roman legionnaires, these dogs wore armor and carried lances strapped to their backs. Molossus hounds were said to be taller than Great Danes and reach weights of up to 280 pounds. These now-extinct giants from the B.C. period aren't completely gone. They're the ancestors of present-day Great Danes and mastiffs.

What's a dog's tail for?

● ● ● ● ● ● ● ●

When it wags, does that mean the dog is happy?

cut

Experts debate whether or not a wagging tail means happiness, but it definitely means excitement. Tails are always a good indicator of how a dog is feeling. An active, upright tail means things are fine, or at least interesting. A slowly twitching, upright tail and a stiff tail held straight out are warning signs, telling us a dog is wary and on guard. A drooping, tucked-under tail means things are really bad. The dog also may crouch

Ring

and make himself look smaller as if to say, "I'm small, don't hurt me." This makes him look sorry, no matter how he actually feels. Tails also act as a balance with a dog's neck, providing a kind of rudder when a dog is running, jumping, or swimming.

There are countless types of tails, including bobtail (Old English sheepdog); crank tail (bulldog); otter tail (Labrador retriever); squirrel tail (Pekingese); flagpole tail (basset hound); rat tail (Irish water spaniel); pothook tail (shih tzu); whip tail (greyhound); curled tail (chow chow); plume tail (pomeranian); ring tail (Afghan hound); sword or saber tail (German shepherd); tufted tail (Chinese crested); sickle tail (Chihuahua); and docked tail (boxer, Doberman). Like docked ears, docked tails are not natural, and seem to be falling out of favor.

Why do dogs sniff under each other's tails?

Dogs don't consider this behavior to be the least bit rude. The smells under a dog's tail tell where he's been, what he's been doing, and how he ranks socially compared to the dog doing the sniffing. A dog has two scent glands, one on each side of his anus, so sniffing under the tail is an ideal spot to find the facts. A dog who is allowed to sniff another dog under the tail is of a higher rank than the dog being sniffed. In other words, the sniffer outranks the sniffee.

Dogs sniff all around each other, but sniffing under a tail reveals the most information.

Do dogs have baby teeth that fall out before they get their adult teeth?

People have 32 adult teeth, including our often removed wisdom teeth. People are usually born toothless, with baby teeth starting to grow in at around six months of age. Those baby teeth fall out when adult teeth grow in, beginning at around five years.

Dogs also are born without teeth. Their puppy, or milk, teeth (28 of them) start coming in at around five weeks. By four months, the puppy teeth are being pushed out and replaced by 42 adult teeth. That includes the four distinctive—and very sharp—canine teeth at the front of the jaw.

Because kids are talking by the age of five, they usually tell their parents when they feel a loose tooth, and they often offer that tooth (for cash) to the tooth fairy. Puppies, on the other hand, tend to swallow their baby teeth, which pass harmlessly through their digestive systems.

Why aren't dogs supposed to eat chocolate?

Theobromine—a primary ingredient in chocolate—is toxic to dogs. It can cause liver failure and even death if dogs eat enough of it. Commercially made chocolate candy, which is loaded with more sugar and milk than chocolate, probably won't make a dog sick unless the dog is quite small. But chocolate can have some nasty side effects. It can cause seizures, vomiting, diarrhea, and hyperactivity. According to the National Animal Poison Control

Center, milk chocolate has 44–60 milligrams of chocolate per ounce. Unsweetened baking chocolate has 450 milligrams per ounce. As little as one ounce of baking chocolate or 10 ounces of milk chocolate can be lethal to a small dog. But no matter what size your dog is, eating chocolate (and, yes, most dogs do have a sweet tooth), is a bad idea.

Keep all chocolate away from your dog, especially if your dog is small.

When your dog stares
at you, he just wants
to know what's
on your mind.

When a dog stares at you, what is he thinking?

He could be thinking about attacking (that's what a wild wolf would be thinking), but it's more likely he's trying to decide what you—a hard-to-understand human being—are going to do next, and, more importantly, what you want him to do.

Have you ever had a staring contest with a friend to see who could go longest without laughing? If you're in a staring contest with a dog, he'll never laugh. But if you win the contest, it just might help him decide who's in charge: you.

What color is a dog's skin underneath all that fur?

Dogs come in all colors. Dogs with darker coats usually have darker skin. Dogs with spotted coats, likewise, have spotted skin. The color of a dog's belly, where there isn't much fur, is often a good indication of the color of his skin. Dogs with pink bellies can even have freckles (on their bellies), just like light-skinned people.

The color of a dog's fur is often a clue to the color of his skin.

Can dogs remember stuff?

· · · · · · · · ·

How long are their memories?

People see something and remember it. Dogs smell something and remember it. There are well-documented stories of l-o-n-g memories in dogs, from Greyfriars Bobby, who lived on top of his master's grave for 14 years until his own death, to Hachi-Ko, an Akita who kept a 10-year vigil in a Tokyo train station waiting for his (dead) master to return. If you've ever seen a movie where the dog recognizes someone (probably the bad guy) nobody else seems to know, that's scent memory at work. And it works.

How many toes does a dog have?

Dogs have four toes on each paw. They have a fifth toe, called a dewclaw, on each of their forelegs, which is sometimes removed when they are four or five days old. The dewclaws of hunting dogs are usually removed because they may catch on bushes and undergrowth. Legend says dewclaws got their name because they don't touch the ground. They merely brush the dew from the grass.

Long ago, dewclaws did touch the ground, like the other four claws, and were used to help hold down prey when a dog was hunting. Over the past thousand centuries, the dewclaw migrated up the leg as dogs did less hunting and more hanging out with people. Like a person's appendix, dewclaws today have lost their usefulness.

Dewclaws are often removed when a dog is four or five days old.

Are the pads on a dog's foot part of his toes?

Footpads are also called toe cushions, and a dog has to have them if he wants to walk and run. Dogs have five pads on each foot—four in front attached to each claw, and one in the middle. Their footpads are insulated with extrathick skin that's less sensitive to heat and cold than the rest of a dog's body, an excellent trait for the part that always touches the ground.

Dogs walk on their toes, not on the soles of their feet like humans. This makes them better suited than we are for running, as they are always in the get-ready, get-set, go position.

The Norwegian Lundshund, a rare breed found only on two islands north of Norway, has eight footpads per foot, a special adaptation (engineered through selective breeding) that allows the Lundshund to scale rocks and catch the island puffins.

Retrievers tend to be
enthusiastic greeters.

Why do dogs seem so happy to see us, even if they've just seen us?

No matter where you've been, even if you've been away for just a minute, you bring back new smells every time you walk in the door. That's one reason your dog is happy to see you.

But the enthusiasm of the greeting depends on the personality of the dog. Some dogs are just naturally bouncy and enthusiastic. They're eager to express excitement at just about anything that happens, including your return from taking out the garbage.

Your dog likes you. He really likes you. Dogs never pretend to like somebody. It's all genuine doggie love. And if your dog really loves you, he's not kidding or putting on an act. He really is happy to see you. Any place, any time.

Why do dogs have cold, wet noses?

Moisture helps conduct scent, and most moist or wet things feel cold to the touch. A dog's cold, leathery nose is naturally moist. But dogs also lick their noses frequently to help their scenting ability.

A dog's whiskers are harder to see than a cat's.

Cats have whiskers. Do dogs?

Dogs have whiskers above their eyes, on their muzzles, and below their jaws, although the whiskers are sometimes almost invisible in their fur. A dog's whiskers are less sensitive than a cat's but still make up an important element in a dog's sense of touch. Whiskers sense airflow, helping dogs know where to sniff for the best information. The scientific name for whiskers is vibrissae.

Why do dogs lick us?

· · · · · · · · ·

Do they wish we'd lick them back?

Dogs lick their own wounds as well as the wounds of pack members. Veterinarians speculate that they do this to keep a wound clean and free of maggots. Throughout history in some civilizations, a dog's lick was considered a healing touch. In ancient Rome, people worshipped Asklepios, the god of medicine. Sick people would go to the Asklepios temples to have the temple dogs try to lick away everything from blindness to tumors.

Clearly, dogs lick people as a way to care for us and show their affection, just as wolves lick their pack members. Dogs wouldn't mind if we licked them back. But since we're alpha members of the pack, they don't expect it.

Dogs, like wolves, show affection by licking their pack members.

Why do some dogs like riding in cars and other dogs don't?

This probably has as much to do with a dog's first experiences in a car as anything else. Was his first car ride a trip to the vet? Did he get shots? Did he get poked and prodded and maybe growled at by other bigger dogs?

If your family takes your dog to fun places, he's sure to love riding in the car!

Does he ever get to ride in the car just for fun? If you consistently take your dog along every time you go out, he's almost certain to love car rides. Besides the feel of the wind in his fur, there are wonderful smells sliding by your car every time your dog sticks his nose out the window, kind of like smell-a-vision. So, if you give him a chance to get used to it, any dog could grow to enjoy the mobility and power offered by a nice, leisurely ride in the car.

How many breeds of dogs are there in the world?

There are over 400 breeds, but some are recognized by only one country's dog or kennel club. A purebred dog (mutts are mixed breeds) has a sire (father) and dam (mother) of the same breed. And his parents both had parents of that same breed, and so on, going back to whenever the breed was developed.

Modern dog breeds were first officially registered, or recorded, in the 1870s in England. Now, there are registering bodies, or dog clubs, in almost every country in the world. In the USA, that registering body is the American Kennel Club, or AKC.

Over 400 breeds of dogs are recognized around the world.

Who was the most famous dog ever?

It's impossible to pick just one. There are dog stars in books, such as Buck in Jack London's *Call of the Wild* and the faithful Argos in Homer's *Odyssey*. There are many more dog stars in the movies and on TV, from Lassie and Rin Tin Tin to Old Yeller and Mickey Mouse's canine sidekick, Pluto.

There are a couple of real-life dogs, however, who have gone down in history and are now best remembered for their amazing courage. Balto is the husky who saved hundreds of people from a diphtheria epidemic in Alaska in 1925 (the famous Iditarod race is based on his run). And Laika is the first dog in space. She went up in the former Soviet Union's *Sputnik II* in 1957. It was a space capsule that wasn't designed for recovery, so Laika never came down. Strelka, however, in 1960, became the first dog to orbit the earth (18 times!) and return safely.

But really, why do dogs like people?

We're circling around to that same old puzzling question. In a world where most animals count human beings as the enemy, how did the precious bond between human and dog take hold? After all, these four-footed playmates and coworkers started out as wolves.

Although it's funny to look at a Chihuahua and a wolf and try to imagine them as relatives, they both have the same genes, the same sociability, and the same instincts. Wolves, however, are wild. Even tame wolves retain a certain amount of unpredictable wildness.

Dogs are wolves we can trust. They're quite different from their genetic twin. Today, we're part of our dogs' packs and they're part of our families. They have come to embrace us as their leaders, helpers, parents, and friends. We each have strengths and weaknesses, and we're each eager to help the other.

Dogs are wolves we can trust. We're part of our dogs' packs and they're part of our families.

Dogs come in many sizes with a variety of skills, from the golden retriever (upper left) to the Chihuahua (upper right) to the greyhound (above).

dog superlatives

FASTEST: greyhound

SLOWEST: basset hound

BIGGEST: mastiff

SMALLEST: Chihuahua

LOUDEST: any dog of any size who won't stop barking

QUIETEST: basenji—they don't bark, but they do yodel

SMARTEST: Border collie

DUMBEST: Afghan hound (Both smartest and dumbest ratings are according to *The Intelligence of Dogs* by Stanley Coren. Note that this measures a dog's intelligence in terms of his ability to be trained to work with human beings.)

HAIRIEST: Old English sheepdog

BALDEST: Mexican hairless

HOTTEST: a dog's normal temperature is 101 degrees Fahrenheit compared to . . .

COLDEST: a person's normal temperature is 98.6 degrees. We're definitely the coldest members of the pack. This is how we got the expression "three dog night." If it's so cold that you have to sleep with three dogs under your covers to keep warm, it's a chilly three dog night.

resources

BOOKS

COREN, STANLEY. *The Intelligence of Dogs: A Guide to the Thoughts, Emotions, and Inner Lives of Our Canine Companions.* New York: Bantam Books, 1995.

THE DOGS HOME BATTERSEA. *A Passion For Dogs.* Devon: David & Charles Publishers, 1992.

DUNLOP, ROBERT, DVM, AND DAVID WILLIAMS. *Veterinary Medicine, An Illustrated History.* St. Louis: Mosby-Year Book, Inc., 1996.

FOGLE, BRUCE, DVM. *The New Encyclopedia of the Dog.* New York: Dorling Kindersley, Inc., 2000.

MORRIS, DESMOND. *Illustrated Dogwatching.* New York: Crescent Books, 1996.

PALMER, JOAN. *Dog Facts.* London: Quarto Inc., 1991.

WILCOX, BONNIE, DVM, AND CHRIS WALKOWICZ. *The Atlas of Dog Breeds of the World.* Neptune City: T.F.H. Publications, Inc., 1995.

YAMAZAKI, TETSU AND TOYOHARU KOJIMA. *Legacy of the Dog.* San Francisco: Chronicle Books, 1993.

WEB SITES

www.akc.org
This is the official Web site of The American Kennel Club. Click on Kid's Corner for a lot of fun and information.

www.avma.org/careforanimals/kidscorner/
Learn from the pros at the Web site of the American Veterinary Medical Association and check out their Kid's Corner.

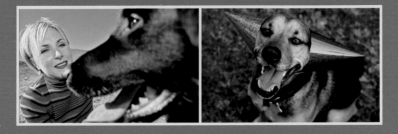

www.barkingbuddies.com
From Australia comes this Web site that includes games, postcards, cartoons, and a free screen saver.

www.canismajor.com
This is a comprehensive Web site that includes breed profiles, veterinary information, current news articles about dogs, and, most importantly, a look at wild canids.

www.ckc.ca/
The Canadian Kennel Club's Junior Kennel Club can be found by clicking on Webster's Place, which has an ongoing, interactive game called Dog Detective.

www.dog-play.com
Log onto this Web site to see what you can do to have fun with your dog.

www.geocities.com/heartland/Plains/9543
For fun, log onto Scooter's Electronic Digs, a Web site that gives you a dog's-eye view featuring a basset hound named Scooter.

www.loveyourdog.com
A dog-loving teacher from California developed this Web site on dog care for kids, which also features readers' dogs, poetry, riddles, stories, careers with dogs, and even a scavenger hunt.

www.ooowoo.com
This site about dog sledding is the place to go if you've ever been interested in mushing.

www.the-kennel-club.org.uk
The official Web site of the British Kennel Club has a Young Kennel Club (YKC) section that's just a click away from the home page.

www.wnet.org/extraordinarydogs/
The public broadcasting station in New York City, WNET, has a Web site for kids called Extraordinary Dogs, which is the result of a documentary of the same name that aired in 1997.

About the Author

AWARD-WINNING AUTHOR MARTY CRISP WRITES books for children and adults. She's also an animal lover and has worked for a veterinary clinic and an animal shelter. In addition to writing books, she is a journalist for the *Lancaster Sunday News* and has interviewed Newbery winner Phyllis Reynolds Naylor, literary legend John Updike, and has even covered concerts by performers such as Britney Spears and N'Sync. Ms. Crisp has four grown children and lives with her husband and their three dogs: Jessie, a Yorkshire terrier; Molly, a cairn terrier; and Sophie, a cavalier King Charles spaniel. If you'd like to know more about Marty Crisp, visit her Web site at **www.martycrisp.com.**